IN THE DOME
OF SAINT
LAURENCE
METEOR

NOEL PEATTIE

IN THE DOME
OF SAINT
LAURENCE
METEOR

NEW POEMS

REGENT PRESS
Oakland, California
1999

To my family and friends.

Also with Regent Press:

Western skyline (poems)

Amy Rose, a novel in four parts

*Hydra and Kraken: the lore and lure
of lake-monsters and sea-serpents*

ISBN 1-889059-76-5

*Manufactured In The United States of America
Regent Press 6020-A Adeline
Oakland, CA 94608*

CONTENTS

ACKNOWLEDGEMENT OF PREVIOUS
PUBLICATION:

"Sun poem": earlier version published as broadside,
    Konocti Books, 1975
"The moth,": earlier version published in *Sipapu*, v. 12,
    no. 1, 1981
"In the dome of Saint Laurence Meteor": *Poetry now*
    (Sacramento), July 1995
"Sunday morning bed poem": *Caprice*, August 1995
"Typical tropical trees": *Hammers*, no. 11, June 1996
"I am in bed!" and "Triumphant! happy!" *Poetry now*
    (Sacramento) v. 3, no. 7, July, 1997
"Rondel'ing they mark": *Poetry now* (Sacramento), v. 3,
    no. 1, November 1997
"Sing! shout! clap!": in *Poetry motel*'s "Wallpaper
    series", December 1997
"How to prevent the war of 1812" and "Structure of the
    human I": *Poetry now* (Sacramento), v. 4, no. 3,
    March 1998
"O, catalog girls!": *Cayo*, v. 5, no. 1, summer 1998
"Offering": *Purple* (Park Hills, MO) 26 Oct. 1998
"As they should have assured him": *Mockingbird*, no. 7,
    Spring 1999
"Ode on a not-too-distant prospect": *Poetry now*
    (Sacramento) v. 5, no. 2, February 1999
"&,": *The Ampersand*, v. 17, nos. 3 &4, Autumn/winter
    1998 [arrived 14 Apr. 1999]
"Mortal valley": *Purple* (Park Hills, MO) April 1999

OFFERING

Friends, from here I offer you
my latest
hypnagogic vision:

between green hips,
knees, elbows of hills, —
a ribbon of old cement
mended with asphalt
wandering somewhere
south of west;

no more than one oak tree,
one pickup, one buzzard;
but many the yip-yip-yoos
of night's coyotes
under spring-toppled Orion

    & the bird-quick flash of her smile
    &
    the rise of her breast

that far from the sea fog,
the book-guarded hearths,
the poets' pavements,
of San Francisco.

ON OPENING THE FIRST WINDOW IN SPRING

Air, for the bedroom.
Rain, sickness?
all past.
A view of the road, passing trucks,
green hills;

a maiden skyline,
clear of cloud,
– *I'll* never climb.

CLIP!

the skeleton in spring
(clip) (clip)
patchy brown (clip)
of the branch Ezequiel clipped this morn-(clip)
ing (clip) (clip)
snipped the buds,
buds, buds! which will soon re!
generate!! providing (just
one more [clip: dead twig]) and THEN:

> *if the long shoots go not to the fire*
> *the plant wilds, — sprouts tangledly, —*
> *there is no hope of saving, sweetness, —*

first small green leaves, — come!
next, gold-orange flowers,

finally, glorious messy
seed-laden September
GLOBES!
from our pome-
granate {window}

holy tree.

Not too
close! says the
spider not too
close! to the globe
lamp (a sun suspended,
like her from the ceiling
socket) but clinging waits
instead for the welcome
wandering fly
— or moth —
★

★

as the
poet
waits
for the web
shy reader of
(the perhaps)
this
time
per
fect
★

★

poem
|
★

MEMORY PEBBLE

the pebble on the path
she showed me —
scar-worn by passing
hiker-boots —
went into her remembering bag:
it's there! She keeps the field guide
to all that wings away

FEBRUARY

today in the market
a baby girl w/earrings
ahead of me in checkout line
wouldn't smile in:
no english / maybe spanish

but coming home:
                    Mariani's
earliest almonds
only planted in
                    August

a one/two flowers   now!
on two/three saplings

THE MOTH,

having lived
under the folding back seat of the car,
all the way to San Francisco, —

once the seat was opened, —
she flew out.

O! My!
Is this another world?
How sea-fog-clear the air!
O! coffee-houses! bookstores!
printers! jazz! poets
reading aloud
their immortal crazy poems!
O paradise! O beckoning brilliant
City Lights!

O! San Francisco!

IN BRICKYARD COVE

ripples incoming
pattern / sunlight
— afternoon harbor

shower / sable
stern / there!
— venerable "woodie"

— golden tribute:
ever-falling
mirror-sparks.

AS THEY SHOULD HAVE ASSURED HIM

Monsieur Van Gogh, you are cured.
It is no longer necessary for you
further to endure this asylum.

Your painting of irises, — all violet save one white,
flourishing their green leaves,
wild
        as they drank the blood of fallen martyrs, —

proves you are healthy,
            healthier than many doctors.

Monsieur Van Gogh,
you are this hospital's
master physician:
it is you who have cured us
of all our secret maladies
with your art.

Monsieur Van Gogh! in professional gratitude:

we are shaping you a new,
a prophetic!
ear.

AT LAST

At last, heat breaks,
west wind
-o!w's
road-slice
past mailbox:
slips, blows:
blind flares, rugs flut
-ter

t' wind's westing:
leaves plastered
'gainst screens, fan
whirls b' wind
power,

&!

be-
yond slate-blue
Coast
Ranges,
after-sun
down!
is pale-
gold.

SONATINA

O sea-wind, joy of you,
blind-blower, blanket-bed-
causer, window-fan-
rouser, sleep-easer, in-fall-
rain-bringer, Ocean's child
messenger, speaking:

> *(in solo flute:*

>> as, when
>> ever we bring
>> cool hands to a fore
>> head, drink to a
>> morning
>> cat) —

> for your

stray-blowing, un-
expected in-walking,
relief against summer siege-
stifling,

> joy of you,
> joy of you!

HOLDING ON

The bubble of warm air
that broadened over our dry
October, has boarded a flight
for Boise, ID;
             by way of Reno.

                              Rain,

by Pacific Express, arrives
at 5 a.m., and stops awhile;

flops into the easy landscape,
makes itself at home! patters
about the place — a good aunt, a nurse,
cleaning up, clearing away,
bringing relief to low fever.

How long we can all hold on
with yet another season; the war news
in the paper, mortal illnesses of friends,
the light of the oncoming
tunnel-years —

                     is not a question
to ask the unthinking cat,
who!
(fed, let out, let in) is now
carefully
cleaning his crotch
at the foot
of his morning
bed.

LAST OF THE GREAT POT SALES

The sign on the college town telephone pole said:
"LAST OF THE GREAT POT SALES"
and I didn't go.

The young potters had offered other pot sales before,
and I hadn't gone,
and this last, final, ULTIMATE, chance,
I missed.

They were taking (I heard) their pots away.
They were leaving the kiln,
they were packing up their bedding,
his shirts, her bra, their love. And they were filling
the back of the pickup with:

the unsold coffee cups, the unsold
plates, jars with lids and earthenware ele-
phants out of Zen and Bernard Leach. And their
arguments, and the jug wine, and
the glorious nights with friends:

Zoe and Lynn and Stan and Stacey
and Tom and Will and Joyce and Sinbad the Sailor
and all the kilns and ills and films and pills,

aye, ages long ago, these lovers fled away
in a Toyota pickup truck,
off to New Mexico. Where the skies are cleaner and the
earth is right and everyone else is into pots or turquoise
jewelry or Anasazi patterns
anyway,

and anyway, you and I never knew them. We never slept
with Wilda with her dark green eyes. We never got a
farewell letter from Joyce's curly hair. We never disagreed

23

with princess Zoe about soft porn, —

     at one in the morning.

The '40's and the '50's and the '60's,
and the '70's and the '80's, and the '90's —
have blown away like thistledown. At the university,
no one remembers

any
more.

And the discussions, are wrack lost! on the Farallones.
And being young, is a balloon in a Sacramento norther.
And I will never find them in New Mexico,

for there are no more gold-hatted lovers,
and no more red-hot mamas,

and no more Great Pot Sales.

THE TROTSKYITES

set up their tables:
on springtime quads at
universities; under
summer porticos of co-ops.

They push, thrust,
The Militant, Spartacist,
Workers' Vanguard,

on you! on me! — passing too close
on the bourgeois *trottoir* (they
rival each other; quarrel, divide),
yet urge us to subscribe.

ISMS! — fill their working hours —
none we ever dream of
(though we all buy into
one of them)

and after all, who *was* theoretically correct
in that last battle for Barcelona?
(& their ferocious hero
is surely deep in Mexico's
black volcanic dust)

A PAINTING OF ATLAS

The elderly (two strokes) painter
who comes to paint (a heart attack)
my landlord's house next door
works carefully. S l o w l y.

He speaks country, simply,
with a touch of Irish. We talk
of weather, honest things.

High Culture is a child's
domino tower
on a silver tea-table.

But Bill is an Atlas.
Working expertly,
as usual,
he bears all our civility
on his slender
shoulders.

RUSSIAN POSTCARD

I identify with this hero.
Saffron-armored,
on a persimmon-colored horse,
Ilya will slay
                 the snake from the mountain.
Three-headed dragons *must* die,
for the sake of the village,
even if they emit puffs of smoke,
like a small steam engine, going pfutt, pfutt,
pfutt, as restored
by the Antique Mechanics' Club.

But wait, must Zmeyà Gorinich die?
Perhaps his puffs are synchronized
to operate in sequence!
Might not Ilya Muromyets harness him
to plow the soil of the Motherland,
like a Soviet tractor?

Ah, no:
          for the dragon is not Russian.
He is German, French,
or even American.
He cannot be allowed
                      to spout his flames
on the red soil of Holy Russia.
Die,
       he must.

It is good to be Russian,
to wear a conical helmet,

and to sweep free
the broad land
of serpents, Tatars,
fascists,
          and oppressors.

IN THE DOME OF SAINT LAURENCE METEOR

Meeting the Mexican
boys under Perseids
waving a flashlight
(they'd read the paper)
"you here too?"

yellow stars shattering
blue of Aquila,
indigo Serpens,
dome powdered silver:
— whose wings were those?

— *murciélagos*
dance just above us,
chasing mosquitoes
ere moon-late-rising:

"and are they dangerous?"
"only in Mexico!"

hour before midnight,
feast of Saint Laurence,

this Tenth of August.

OMEN

Just after sundown, bigness of a hazelnut
held at arm's length, head of that star was:
but its long beard stretched half-a-yard against

our autumn skies;
                and some said they saw heads it,
bloody Turks', Christians'; swords, axes, spears.

Then third evening after, All Saints':
out of its crest came a spike, turned a spout
from which poured a sparkle of blood-red stars:
don't you dare doubt it!
                I, even I,
myself! witnessed a piece of cold iron
struck from the smithy which God let the Devil
play with up there:
                iron, yes, fallen
in Trinity churchyard.

                In carts, carriages,
people came from all over the duchy to look at it;
some said folk had seen our star
's far north as Sweden.

What did it mean?

Some said our cattle would all die of the rinderpest.
Others said the Turk would come — see his curved
scimitar out of the head of the hairy star;

but the Turk did not appear. And before the first frost, the
star
                dipped below the horizon,

                horrid beard of him

                              sliding beneath

                                        the Goat.

Yet the star must have foretold something:

In January, fell the heaviest of snows
in half a hundred years;
                              and when spring broke,
robbers, hurters of women, evil men
(God shame them, punish them!) gathered,
up there, in the mountains,

the dangerous passes.

REMEMBERING WORLD WAR TWO

We huddled around headlines, around
the radio boxed in the dark,
safe but not too young
to be sorta scared:

Pearl-gray ships heeling
over. Enemy subs poking up
off both our coasts. Enemy
flags, gorgeously evil.
Marine pilots in uniform,
confident,
welcomed to the house.

LIFE showed us Coral Sea, Midway,
pushed the danger back to the Solomons:
we felt safer, still followed the war
as a gigantic, terrible game.

We were so deafened by headlines
that we could not hear:

tail fins, hot tubs,
Korea-Vietnam,
approaching in the distance,

and the shots fired by
young men in
our own uniforms
at Kent State.

ODE ON A NOT-TOO-DISTANT PROSPECT

The Y2K approaches! the terrible
Two Thousand year: when every computer crashes,
all power shuts down, planes skid, traffic lights go dead.
The moms and dads and sons and sisses
and cats and dogs run out of their houses,
battling each other with golf clubs
for the last cheeseburgers and chocolate milk shakes,
while cars stall on the freeway and
the National Guard *can't* get through,
'cause the tanks won't start.
It's coming up from Futureland,
                like a swarm of killer bees!

Only the survivalists are even half prepared.
See them bedded down with their doxies,
in their root cellars, making babies:

rifles within reach, kerosene lanterns aglow,
Douglasfir logs cross-stacked against January snows,
fortified, yes!
                by potatoes in boxes, crates of onions,
garlic and chilis strung above their lovebeds,
bottled water from Idaho, cartons of powdered milk,
stacks of old L. L. Bean catalogs,
Countryside and Small Stock Journal,
&,
an apparatus for making moonshine:

ant-like, prudent, defiant; amid
                barrels of dried peas.

"old man grapevine"

old man grapevine & his brothers
close-trimmed — weather-bent —
warding ranch's south frontier
in February-cold sunlight —

yet their sons will all be
lords of *Muscat* —
and their sweet daughters
prides of *Alexandria*

SPRING AFTERNOON

I sit in the spring afternoon,
while the rain troubles all of the leaves,
and the thunder bowls away.

The dove calls alow, low, low, low,
and the thunder stumbles away.

JACKRABBITS AT NIGHT

Escorted (it may be to my grave!) by jackrabbits,
jumping out at me, into the headlights
like crazy quarterbacks down into the ditch
for a forward pass, I never pass; their 40-
yard line is just west of Interstate 505. I'm

the cautious runner, up front and down
the middle. Nothing the Jacks ever learned
(will rabbits ever learn?) prepared them for
two glaring lights at 50 miles an hour. No
diagrams in their book; no book; no side-
lines medic for an injured Jack. Let them

race, run, fall behind, drop into the ditch and away!
Not to swerve to avoid their deaths, slam brakes,

                                        skid:

thus I'm well content with the score:

Jacks 6, poet 1.   We beat the odds
once more.

SPRING RAIN

rainrain

      rain
           rainrain
  rain   rain

     rainrainrain   rainINGrain

          INGrainagain

   raining   rain still
        sparrow
                rain
sparrow rain

     rain   rain rainINGrain
            sparrow

sparrowsparrowsparrow *sparrow sparrowsparrow* <u>up</u>!!

EARTHEARTH EARTH pool/ EARTHEARTH
earth   earth   •drops•   earth   earth

36

DAWN

                    W I N D O W

                       a
                  b   ckbird
                  l
  F   F
                     finch
                     finch
  R   finch   R

                    S A S H

  A   finch   A
                  sparrow

         dove DOVE dovedovedove

  M   ea   M
                  h   s
                  p   ant!
         dove DOVE dovedovedove
  E   E

              S I L L   S I L L

  B E D
                                      CAT.

LATE FALL IN BIG VALLEY

Dawn twilight: gray winter feather-
light on the bed. Somewhere,
out there, maybe overhead, —
sounds: like a distant-faint skein
of geese, honking, talking,
calling, in their sailing
through our plain sky. I've seen them
daytimes;

                they don't always seem
to know in which direction they should be
going: northing in winter? silly geese!
or maybe they've found another bulldozed pond
(there's one here, end of the big field;
a wild-goose chase away, I've never seen).

Wetlands for waterbirds! This fall-brown heartland
valley is big: nearly old England's length:
four hundred miles from Red Bluff down!
south! to the Grapevine. Are those geese confused?
Perhaps they're honking, searching, for the
Pleistocene lake that filled the San Joaquin.

Ice bestrode the Sierra, slicing Dome in Half;
Stockton an island for reeds and nesting ducks;
the night that old mammoth slipped, fell, drowned
in our Cache Creek. Wet enough, that year, for
support of a superparliament of fowls.

Or maybe it wasn't dawning geese, only a diesel
engine starting up, at five to furrow the land.
Or domestics, neighbors' geese; wings clipped:
property!

Our land: with few ponds for wild-waders:

mostly drained
for crops and houses: filling now with golden

at-last-real-get-up-working-morning-light.

FOR TWO FRIENDS IN MAINE

In Maine, where I have never traveled,
two friends, in different country towns, sit
in sunlit armchairs wedged between
Canada and the Atlantic Ocean.
Over their heads float the Stars and Stripes;
and on the flagpole they've attached a sign,
        "MAINE, 1820:
but American much longer than that."

First thing out of bed,
my friends put on their oilskins,
rush down the road to the harbor,
clear the stile at a single bound,
and haul the Sun out of the sea:

it's red and dripping,
they wash the spots off its face
(some of them don't come off)
then let it bob loose, gently, up in the sky,
to shine over the rest of us in America.
Then they sit down, their duty done,
to buckwheat cakes and fried salt cod.

My friends have it all under control,
      up there in Maine.
And should ever our country's peace be threatened,
they'd haul out the old cannon
(abandoned by Arnold's expedition)
from the woodshed:

swab the rust out of the barrel,
load it with black powder,
ram down a ten-pound ball,
and fire it!!!
              at whatever hostile sail

dared to approach the rocks, the pines,
the blueberries,
and the harmless ambling cows

of Maine.

HISTORY POEM

General Ambrose Burnside USA ordered my
great-grandfather, Frederick Wilkinson, with
Michigan Second, Poe's Brigade, up Marye's Heights;
Fredericksburg, 13 December 1862. Barksdale's
Mississippi Brigade drove them all back.
He was wounded; news reached Kalamazoo
that he was dead. His daughter Elia,
born prematurely, lived to write for the newspapers,
published several novels, birthed four children.
But her father survived, built houses
in Pasadena.
General Burnside was thrice
governor of Rhode Island, viewed
the Franco-Prussian War from the German side,
died in office as a Senator.

Twenty years later:
at night my great-grandmother heard her husband,
neurotic, irritable,
waking from a troubled dream:

"The guns. I hear them. The guns, I can't
stop hearing them.
The guns."

IF ... (A TRANSLATION)

I am escaped from the perfidious
English, but only to a state
where no one speaks any French
but bad. I have a commission
of general from this Madison, but —
he gives me no command. I sit
writing letters he does not answer,
drinking rum, rum,
rum, what else? — in an old house
in *la Nouvelle Orléans*. The flies
of winter, the mosquitoes of summer
exercise continually my (two sole) aides.
(The slaves, although by the
government provided, are
useless). — I find in myself a pain
in my stomach,
the wine here is far from good;
I couch myself after dinner
and read Euripides in French.
My body I rub with ice from the Ohio.
I bore myself; there are no enemies
here, save the distant Kiowas, to fight.

It would have been for me far better
to have fallen, tricolor in hand,
before the frozen walls
of burning Moscow.

HOW TO PREVENT THE WAR OF 1812

Occupy Bermuda,
the Royal Navy's forward base,
— just the beach,
please, of course.

Bring barbecue fixin's,
charcoal, lighter fluid,
chicken, small spicy sausages,

tossed green salad,
thin-sliced tomatoes, cleaned shrimp,
ranch dressing,

umbrellas, suntan lotion,
bikinis, sunglasses,
volleyball, net, and two poles,
and
little painted tin pails and shovels
for the kids.

When the Royal Navy arrives
to reclaim their island,

invite them ashore for

LUNCH! From the big keg
in the wet sand,
pour them
a cold beer.

They'll understand. Let it all hang out.
Talk it over. It'll
all work

out.

RIGHT!

Right through the right middle of the view
from the recliner a phone pole bisects
just right now hour before sundown
the zigzag way a streamstorm
right-left-rights between
sloping agreeing hills quarreling clouds

l i g h t n i n g

to join an irrigation channel that
makes possible
summerstormwater,

neighborly alfalfa,
closer wheat,
and the innocent

!glory¡

of spreading
California
poppies.

I AM IN BED!

I am in bed! annuitant,
on a Wednesday
morning! Beyond the window
the trees wave slowly
and (short-sighted) form
(as I am) circles of pin-hole
images of their rising God:
Sun.

My feet point north. I
rest and read poetry.
I am a meridian line
on a whirling globe. Find me
quick west of Reno,
east of San Francisco, —

but far below my back,
away down there rolls
unsounded, fundamental,
white hot, under
enormous pressure,
Earth's molten iron
core.

SUNDAY MORNING BED POEM

Stretched out obliquely, narrow as Palawan island,
I lie on my side in bed.
The cat has ascended Mount Hip,
and crouches there, waiting.
It will do him no good to wait,
for I am ready:

only to hear the dove call,
to sleep again,
and to dream the next love.

SING! SHOUT! CLAP!

Down in many darkgreen islands
they gather together
every Sunday
as the Sun bronzes the sea:

it's warm in the church,
so they let the trade-winds
stream through:

they SING! they SHOUT! they CLAP!
they WARN! they PRAISE! they MOURN!
and free now
(at least on Sundays)
they get together afterwards,
drink something soft,
watch the children, and
socialize a little.

God, in his Carib hammock,
allows himself a little rum
to *his* fruit juice,

while listening,
very respectfully,
to the tall Pastor's
serious
sermon.

TYPICAL TROPICAL TREES

morning:
she puts out bread crumbs
for the restaurant birds;

Antillean bulfinches
red-throated with desire
profit by her tenderness

later:
I stumble after her, seeking
in towering forests
yellow bananaquits,
green parrots,
her red curls

our rowboat up
the Indian River:
she sees mangroves, mahoganies;
says: "typical tropical trees"

after lunch:
the Rastafarian appears round the
corner of the hotel:
smiling, scared,
sells her four fresh grapefruit

swimming, snorkeling:
white rum, gold almond oil
rubdowns

at bedtime: Canopus
star of the south
rises between our
soft white clouds:
steady as faith:

as she (work-weary
happy-tired now)

sleeps

GREAT WHIM

Estates and fortunes were gambled away:
now only the gecko, twenty
fingers (keeping no score
of the planters' losses; they
drunk as Danes, and he safe on the louvers!)
scurries:

      Great Whim, great house,
still an ellipse, three
great
rooms. Madeira in crystal,
Herr Governor's punch. A game of *skat*.

                  Cannon stare
seaward over the quiet
anchorage, grackles chatter
in the salt-wind-stricken graveyard:
there they all are: and, —
Serfina, who was here in the house to serve.

Was it her, then? still indignant,
she follows us everywhere;

Hurricane Lady, Taino-African,
whom we dread encountering
every year,

in great heat,
           torrential rain,
                    enormous wind:

emblem: a spiralled crushing footprint;
attribute: ruin-haunting gecko;
Unroofer of Estates, Filler of Island
Cemeteries, —

you're the "Great Whim",
whose mothers' mothers' copper-colored people

who (having heard *all!*

                from the Lucayans)

                        greeted

Columbus and his band with a stinging

shower of arrows.

IN THE CLOUD FOREST
(Madagascar)

The malachite kingfisher
on the stump
             by the waterfall
is as
neatly
     placed

as the frog
        on the leaf

letting you

dream

he's a leaf

BLUE ROOM POEM

I was taking a nap in the Blue Room
alone
      (where the cross-currents of
sleep are still shallow
and its waves bring up
sea-drift
      of the mind)

when the landward breeze from the Delta
came up and rustled the window
shade

and I thought it was you,
reading a magazine

why, surely it was you,
my sweet,
there beside me!

(and I was just getting ready
to kiss your smooth shoulder ...)

THE TRUE, THE BLUSHFUL

O garden-hose-fount of water,
clearer than crystal,
through me you bring:

mercy to the late-summer-
flowering bulbs,
cascades for the goldfish
in their outdoor tank,
cool summer drink for the cat.

Long may you readily flow:
abundant as faith, and not

     as when twice in the Middle Ages,
     Pacific rains dried up.

     A fickle god twisted a faucet; Sierra runoff failing,
     so died our
     fresh rivers: nor streamed down to the

     undrinkable, thundering Ocean.

     This valley turned desert.   Folk scattered;
     village to village
     spoke
     dry words

     or none.

What gods they implored for water, I know not.
I pray those Powers, fountain-hose in hand:

may our twenty-meter well not fail;
may I pluck down bursting pomegranates;

&!
may my neighbors make plenty
of crisp white wine,
& true, blushful red, —

for a feast, then a nap, with my sweetheart.

FISHBOWL UNIVERSE

If the bowl we seek an escape from,
— nosing around the glass,
seeing the looming shapes; —
if the bowl widens, opens, streams out,
and the air goes under,
and the clear crystal water
becomes the world, —
will the shapes we now see
beyond the glass,
drown? or bob up endlessly,
flotsam we can ignore?
Or will they turn out just
one of us, waiting to join us,
one of our tribe?

If the bowl we see
is the huge blue bowl of summer,
under it trees, dogs, magpies;
if the turkey buzzards
only rise highest to the distant surface;
and if the cool air widens
at night to take the stars home, —
is not the light past Sagittarius
same as the light on the bookcase?

And the tribes beyond our bowl:
are they not also
guessing at the nature of
the Master of the House?

an elderly, muttery gentleman,
celibate, a fellow of habit, —
fond of his many pets,
his mysterious keys,
indecipherable volumes,

mail from just about everywhere,

his carafe of water,
his bedtime lamp?

COUNTING

"I've met many a farmer,"
said the international
agronomist,
"who couldn't read;
but I never met

>   *one!*

who couldn't count."

In the past 48 hours
the corn has grown
too high!
to let me see the white mail truck
coming north on Road 88.

Let x be the daily rate of the corn's growth:
how many hours, then

(of irrigation, sunlight,
Mexican music from waterers'
pickup trucks)

how many churling blackbirds,
jackrabbits and pheasants
hiding in the Goliath stalks
before that maize obscures the Coast Ranges?

and how many weeks before it's harvested:
slashed and levelled
only to feed our neighbors' stock?
our people?

AT CODY'S,

bought daily ration:
liter of good white wine:
(made this possible).

Fellow next-before me,
old farmer,
liked to talk a little:

I, — that's me, —
showed him Phillips's logo:
strong redhead woman, hauling
huge grape-bunch: slung over back:

told him, "either she's
more-than-exploited,
or she's
stronger than anyman going".

looked at me, eighty summers
farming in Winters, face plowed
as you'd expect (sun-brown eyes)

"what'd you say
you'd stepped in?"

INCIDENT NEAR THE PORT OF OAKLAND

Men, aboard tugboat pushing with a rigid line
Korean freighter, Hyundai-car-laden
to Port of Oakland, watched
(as Korean deckhands, knowing little [if
any] English) stood by as their
(captain doubtless much the same) turned
freighter 15° to starboard, t'avoid
buoy / small boat / or imagined
obstruction, or real: when

line being stiffer than rigor
mortis (turn your living hand
85° on your wrist) their tugboat's hull,
decks: warped all-too-obedient! tilt:
drawn down, sea their stack
drenching, dousing their diesel,
their deckhouse crushed:
now prison
of their unanticipated
drowning: — being dead.

None of this was visible
outside the Port of Oakland,
but this failure of tongues
between two lettered peoples:

 (and did some executive's order
leave them without interpreters?
he sleeps well, no doubt, in bed);

left the daylit blinds
of several working mourning women,
drawn-down

instead.

INVESTMENT

(this poem is not for vegetarians)

Black Angus beeves, raised
for neighbor rancher's future coins, — these,
his cattle: have stopped moaning. The last one
who lowed all night, like one of H. G.
Wells's dying Martians in its tower,
has given up its mindless blaring power.

Shouting "Watch out!", across a half-mile field:
I warned his herd: "Hey, Hamburger!
Chateaubriand, *messieurs*! — that's you! — with *sauce
béarnaise;* or thin-smoked Bœuf
Tartare — you staked-out steaks!
You'll soon be very Tender, Loin!"

"Uh-oh!" (they bellowed back). "No hope!"
Under a fat and prosper moon, their groaning's
ceased with dawn. Only my protein-laden fridge
shuts off and on.

Moon rises higher, a well-thumbed pocket coin.

TRIUMPHANT! HAPPY!

In every county many ranches,
on every ranch, a pickup truck,
and in the back of every pickup,
a dog.

See the pickup trucks
on their lawful occasions:
off to the hardware store,
on a trip to another field,
delivering fertilizer,
visiting another ranch,
and always, in the back of the pickup,
the waving tail of the dog.

The tail beats every second:
watch it as the pickup
bounds along dirt:
stops at another dog's ranch
(courtesies are exchanged);
occasionally, irresistible,
a jackrabbit crosses the field of view
and the rancher whistles the dog back.

All over our county,
the tail wags the pickup.
Follow that dog's tail
to Brooks, Davis, Dunnigan,
Esparto, Guinda, Rumsey,
Winters, Woodland,
Yolo, and Zamora.
Over our brown dirt, our cattle-
nibbled hills,

through orchards and suburbs,
hail it advancing! The tail arrives,
comet-like! triumphant! happy!
The glorious, plumed, adventurous
tail of that dog!
      in the back of the pickup!

STILL LIFE, AND MORE

Two eggs on a wrinkled
paper sack — a bottle, wavy lines of wood
behind it — pears in a silver ewer
sleeping — more bottles, a roll of marbles,
loosed from an old cigar box —

all things round or square,
backed by the most neutral
gray or brown as November, thus
best to display

spoon, feather, shell,
flask, hollow tile,
each in their radiant trance:

the gleam of the ordinary.

DOVE AT YOUR WINDOWS

1

William Leddra, Quaker martyr
hanged on Boston Common, 1661
just for returning to Puritan Massachusetts, —
said he was a
                    "dove at your windows";

I have doves near my windows
all summer long
I am no martyr;

but another summer storm is coming;
and an old farmer I met today
said "it's gonna be like this
all summer long;"

the clouds raise white hands over the hills
the wind rises, stirs the T-shaped props
that we braced under the branches
of the greatly-laden
                              almond tree ...
bearing its green-children

2

and as it turned out
he was wrong for weeks
and weeks;
it got up to a hundred
most of the time

and the doves
are getting along
just fine.

STRUCTURE OF THE HUMAN I

1

The rods are for dark,
and the cones are for light.

The cones love yellow,
but the rods pale green.

If a white star blooms
near a red star,
the white one greens in abundance.

As the red star fades,
it turns gray,
then vanishes.

2

White stars are young;
four in Orion
are old but a hundred
thousand years, —

the time the human race was formed,
when you and I were born,

when scared (round fires) we began to tell
hero-stories in the starlit dark.

TWO NUT POEMS

1

It must be October.
The first walnut
dropped to the roof,
rolled to the edge,
&
landed on the grass, —

ready to eat.

2

With what joy
two magpies and a crow
(who'd scattered at my approach)
flew down to the fragments
of a black walnut I crushed for them
with the wheels of my speeding car.

TWO NOVEMBER RAIN POEMS

1

Fresh scent of
morning rain;

at last.

and just yesterday!

all the firewood, — I, alone, —
stacked under dry shelter.

2

This November rain —

a large number
of very small creatures

stepping and crapping
all over the walkway

in the later evening
dark.

ANTHILL

A small desert fortress, a ring-finger's length in diameter;
built up of earth, from a crack in the earth.

Its people are amazons, clad in sable armor;
each one is nester, robber, soldier.

All day they go in and out, they begin expeditions,
(they have never seen the clouds,
they know nothing of music),
they come home laden with something tiny, edible;

in great heat, in weariness, ancient knights
in dusty helmet, cuirass, greave, —
they gravely salute each other,
silent, obedient:
                           to plunder,
to guard their hoard; to feed
their hidden Queen,

all day, all day.

BETWEEN TWO PEAKS

Between two peaks, an easy-dipping valley
trails down into a huge tangled country:
it's brush, head-high, you have to crawl and struggle
and go through all its scratchy spaces,
working your way in
but though you tire, and have no real hope of
getting through, you have to follow it downward
toward the outside or maybe there's just deer trails
for something you have lost you half-remember
a golden ring, a caring heart, a surcease

it is a sphere called childworld, a land called dying;
            we must explore it

occasionally at night I glimpse, I skirt

            its borders ...

NIGHTSOUNDS

The fridge shuts on and off.
A nut rolls off the roof.
Eleven p. m. arrival
of a pickup,
at the ranch across the road.
This centenarian wooden farmhouse
chills down,
                 calms down.
No worse thumps than those.

But, surely,
a gigantic elephant,
over in Africa,
stamps,

           and the sound of his forefoot,
muffled through miles of earth,

is a faint warning thump of dread,
to me,
in the dark,

in bed.

LISTENING

Four a.m.;
tail end of the storm,
rolling-away of night.

The drainpipe from the gutter
gurgles to the pebbles,

explains it all
to the cat.

Yes.

So who else out there
is
listening?

Into the middle of the green
the mind, that runs up trees, pretends
the world starts, where the roofline ends,
then scrambles, to where blue is seen.

The mind's a squirrel; your ifs and buts
neglects for love-chasing in leaves;
strange opportunity it sees
to search for not-yet-opened nuts.

The leaves work harder than the mind.
They take light till the sun has set
and blue has turned to violet,
and Moon's a yellow lemon rind,

then rest. The mind delights to stray;
and, never finished with its streaming,
spends half the night in wastrel dreaming,
from leaf to bole, from work to play.

A world's rogue flower is a mind.
In common life it strikes a root,
then blossoms hugely, to dispute
the power of seed of other kind;

then fades, then withers, then is seen
fallen and scattered, and will blow
the way the almond petals go,
into the middle of the green.

THE GREAT SERBONIAN BOG

(mentioned by Pliny and Milton)
is quite impossibly im-
passible; fed by Nile
languidly, 's no more
than fathom twain in depth:

save where Typhon's springs,
hot, tepid, bubbling murky, keep it
glurping full, even when-
ever-distant mountains' torrents fail
or sink
in early sand. Its

shallow
waters shelter
huge skeins of skittering, wintering
waterfowl; there

tall herons with enormous
beaks stare into pools
as philosophers into ancient
books.

      The meaning of it all?
eludes the fools with guns, whom
Father Mud devours. (Whole
armies, JM says, have dis-
appeared there [Publius Rufus, stop
pushing, my boots are ...]) Boats, stuck, rot, —
worms' food.

      By jetliner,
seeing no farms, nor towns,
thórough the morning fog,
the thirty-thousand-foot-high passengers

drift off!
sleep.

I remind (at bedtime)
myself that while *bog*
in English means a dangerous muddy hole,
in Danish it means "book", and in Russian
(there, too, pronouncéd slightly differently)
it resembles their
word for
God.

MORTAL VALLEY

Endlessly your shock-tired wagons rumbling downway
    from heartbreaking passes,
yielding their felloes to branches, break-axle boulders,
    as body to labor, thirst, hunger, weakening, sleep,
 death. The rattlesnake bajadas first lose juniper,
    sagebrush; then next, the skulking chollas
jumpy with fishhook thorns; lastly, a huge ochre vista
    opens: a dusty, empty shroud;
once living lake: now locoweed saltpans.

    At the lake's former bottom
you'll find a spring, foul as a black fart,
    sulfur and poisonous oxides.
Well, you wanted it, this is where you slipped
    down through your lifeways;
took wrong passes, ignored help-voices, found scouts shot
    only when wheels broke:
poor soft oxen collapsed, betrayed, led into
    no green pastures, no still waters.
Man, who will lead now! So little time left, afternoons
    withered,
    night full of stars, stars, stars!! overhead sparkling
Vega reminds you: your whole life shrivels to

    here.

&:

as in the D &
R G W / Rail. Road.
(Dangerous, &
Rapidly Growing Worse).
(But the view from the windows,
they say, is gr&).

&, a c&didate for Congress,
seated at his table,
offering his brochure,
with the welfare cuts he's pl&.

&, shapeless, accusing,
the h&s-out homeless person
seated on the sidewalk:
& she will be your judge
when the workers rule the l&.

Nurse & aide,
dem&ing you hold still for a
giant hypodermic:
which is more than you can
st&.

&, finally, the bald
& inevitable &
ubiquitous dart-bearer, who

points an end
to &s.

.....!!

      [pheasant alarm!]

a watchman's rattle,
cry!
      patrolling

        the green wheatwall:

ring-necked chief,
dun hen followers:
he mounts one,
treads her, — joy!

       struts on.

Soldiers in the heat,
men at sea, in bitterest weather,
mothers four flights up,
drunks downtown,
tired librarians and teachers, kids
frightened at school, prisoners;
the dying,
and the watchers there;

all, all, would rather watch the green wheat
growing,
the pheasant mount his mate,

then be where they are now:
coping with weariness, weather helm, child;
dreading the next hour, tomorrow,
forever?
doomed to hang on,
hold the railings,

wait.

POEM

Where there is overgrown greenness
    let there be cutting and clearing.
Where there are things best forgotten   let there
be gathering and burning.
Where there are dry patches
    let there be planting and watering.
Where there are noises of traffic
    let there be doves and finches.
Where there have been quarrels and heartbreak
    let there be nights of love,

    (Let that Delta breeze arise and come
    this evening),

    nights of love.

POEM 2

The year turns autumn, the canal runs dry.
White egrets circle in a blue-white sky.

o

o little wind I know you
birds easting I follow you!
by clouds spouting slowly
over western skyhills

                    I divine:

And praise!

gardener's altar-bride, walking,
trees' healing-girl, laughing!
after January dry fog-bowl, at last!
this loosing of

tender ... rains

A CLOUDY EARLY MORNING IN AMERICA

Lying in bed listening
as pickup trucks rush by
on the two-lane beyond
the window, and our western
bird-life calling wild

as the colorless dawn
slowly fills the room
with burnished light;

remembering vacation trips
 — highways forty years ago,
with someone kindly
at the wheel —
one of so many!

now dust and shade.

MORNING FALL

September dawn, window west:
plowed ground
amber under returning light.

In the lower sky:
Earth's penumbra,
gray-blue, slides down
(carrying the last planet)

beyond the grass-brown hills.

POEM IN THREE COLORS

October afternoon:

a late-gold light
over all, a distant hay-
baler, swish-
whipping
silver sound, —

and just the slightest
chill in the
air,

the faintest sharp-
warning
gray taste

of smoke.

PARTING

The jaws of the long-
opened pomegranate
hang swaying from its tree,
end of autumn wind —
skull without a brain.

And because I did not pluck its smile,
swallow
its seeds,

its weathered yawn
so deathy now —

is strictly
for the birds.

11 DECEMBER 1996

1

Intense quiet
of early morning
fog.

No bird calls.

In the kitchen window
a daddy-long-legs
clings to a long-dead
fly.

2

In the afternoon, wind
rises, sobs
several keys.

Outside, clouds,
whole continents, lakes,
fortresses and shrouds,
silver-gray,
move, slowly,
before the west wind.

18 JUNE 1997

1

Under a nearly full Moon,
fifteen Black Angus bulls
graze the stubble in a neighbor's field.

Earth's gray half-shadow
rises, backs the Moon-lamp;
makes it shine,
sole golden melon.

The field turns bronze, darkens.
Under that globe,
the cattle are black, barely visible.

2

Two young men
working by electric light
in the doorway of the barn,
put new tires on the go-cart;

they are strong, clever-fingered,
preoccupied.

They turn their muscular backs to the Moon.

O, CATALOG GIRLS!

The catalog girls won't come out tonight:

they're too busy in real silk,
chenille, laughing, wearing
suede, holding puppies,
gloves, watering
flowers, just out of sight of their husbands,
lovers;
some of them are pregnant,

for it's been a lovely summer on Nantucket;
late fall in St. Croix, in clogs on the beach
with the children, in the evenings the tea-
gowns cost one hundred forty-eight dollars,
[who knows/cares what the garment
workers got
out of it all?]
however: their men pay all the bills;

but the sweethearts won't slip off their clothes for us,
for they're only catalog girls:
under their silks and summer knits
nothing that's advertised, nothing *at all*,

to dance by the light of the
Moon.

RONDEL'ING THEY MARK

Crowding on sail, the boat heels fifteen degrees.
There's no way! this race! the helmsman could possibly
        fail:
the crew and tactician can do pretty much as they please,
        crowding on sail.

Look at them, all of them, merry legs dangling over the
        rail,
gallant as kids upside-down on jungle-gyms for a tease.
Wouldn't you like to do that, twenty, and healthy, and
        male?

At that age no flask of *el cheapo* holds any lees.
The clubhouse's cup's the same as the Holy Grail.
They'll never grow old, feel hips giving way, or their
        knees,
        crowding on sail.

MIDMOST OF THE SEAS OF LIFE

Midmost in confused seas
where great tides race
        confronting joined rivers,

I, soaked, wildered! in the small boat,

thought of you clearly, steadily
writing in your yellow house:

two, rounded by the world's
curling, confounding,

whelming winds,
and emerald seas.

O DO YOU REMEMBER ... ?

O do you remember o you must remember
the Avalon Casino where the graduating class
of nineteen-loving-lad-&-lass
danced the subtropical night away
on Catalina!
Santa Catalina
Island!?

And how the big band sound
went around and around
till they
would no more play
without more pay?

O do you remember how we all
went out on the casino's rimming wall
and tried to guess which isle was San Clemente
and which was just L. A.?
And the lights of the town went dim
and every she was unequally
matched with every him?

Can you recall how the star-pouring fall
of the Milky Way appeared beneath the pall
of the rising shadow from the land
and what you tried to do
with your hand?

At long last,
the musicians passed;
it was time to go home.
Fingers might no farther roam.
Only one of us
noticed Sagittarius, —
constellation sparkling,

in night's black hair a silver comb,

sinking, at four A. M.,

beneath Pacific
foam.

SOME SYNÆSTHETIC NOTES

C,
pure spring water,
taste of limestone
surfacing granite;
only a chemist's guess of
minor heavy metals.

G,
homely brown key.
Never buy a used car from
someone who absolutely cannot
(Abe Lincoln could!)
carry a tune in G.

F,
plain-
tive plant-wet
shepherd's plum-
sweet plangent fragrant
piping paradise.

D,
golden key of happiness!
wheat fields, harvest joy!

B-flat,
maids in meadows,
getting gently laid therein,
are by their lovers
admonished, "yield,
be flat. —And they do; and are.

A!
key of geniuses! rapid dazzling
scales by philharmonically &!
excellently exacting violoncellists!

E-flat:
Trumpets, festivals,
sweet processions!

E,
top of the young violinist's
coloratura reportorium.

A-flat,
Hymns, complicated, sonorous,
only for the ancient organist
of Holy Trinity & All Those
Angels.

B,
a thorn-sharp green
wilderness,
full of brambles, berries,
and bees.

D-flat,
A Polish castle
in the fog.
The lovely learnéd châtelaine,
light in the lightened doorway,
will let you love her
iff (=if & only if)
you can count to
one hundred two
in her musical
language.

TROPICAL FISH

swim: swarm:
on: carefully:
squared:
tiles:
red over green:
gold upon turquoise: up
stairs in panels a-
long with voiceless peacocks
in Chinese yellow

you'd think we were in
the tropics!
& so warm already
wait:
'til you see the real
down there tropical fish

meanwhile:
    those brown men in coveralls:

    [Navidad] [Rodriguez] [Pedrillo]

with green sliding hoses
sluicing, with long
brushes cleaning:
                    those tiles
fresh for Santa Barbara's,
Avalon's summers:

all those obedient
tropical fellows
washing those motionless
tropical fish

TO PART IS TO DIE A LITTLE

It's
only mid-July! but the swallows
are fewer this morning, a-
dancing over our bridges;

they're starting to south now,
to plazas, to pampas,
to drowsy belfries with
love-holy names;

all those saints and angels
mourning over gentle altars.

Soon swallows, in south's mid-summer,
will see, skimming over *la cuna*,
donkey, ox; and straw-bedded,
the Infant, safe, by the Mother;

while a hundred votive candles
flame-tremble in adoration,

whenever the church door opens
to the cooler-and-farther-than-

Capricorn wind.

SUNDOWN

Eight pomegranates are lying on the bare ground
in a red circle, where they fell from the tree.
Sundown, and the amber light
signs the fall day's end ...

ENVY

this my sky's
sundown
celadon,

you Koryo dynasty
ceramicists,

for mine was heaven's
showing, frail as a plate, right
here, last evening, and

for two minutes only!
of perfect! palest!
gray-blue-green
last
light.

ROUNDING CAPE FLY-AWAY

(Cape Fly-away — in French, Terre de Beurre, Land of
Butter: at sea, the appearance of land on the horizon,
caused by low clouds at sunset or sunrise [Falconer's
Dictionary of the marine])

When you round Fly-away Cape,
is there safe anchorage at Fiddler's Green?
are there many other boats?
are you hailed, cheerly?
is Mahogany Reef on a rhumb line?
are sea folk, all, jolly,
and the girls jolie, all ways?

are there honies
in the Land of Butter? or
is the appearance of hills at sunset
only low cloud?

and what of the dark?
when, after the new constellations —
Parrot, Pirate, Coins —
tilt silently out of the sea,
and ride through the high south midnight,
is there a new pride of the morning?

or are we, forever:
aground at high tide?

to trust, we have only
the anchor
and the rode ...

EVENING —

the City floods
with the swarming
troops of Night.

Emperor of Dark!
a safe-conduct, please,
through your umbral
armies;

and when I reach dawn's
doubtful morning-
dream-guarded

perimeter,

kindly release me!

just one more time.

WHY THE LOST ONE, AFTER TWO-THREE DAYS, FLEES THE VOICES OF RESCUERS

Because Darkness is a country and the Moon
is the Speaker of its House.

Because Water, wild, is cold.

Because Bruises recall past Injuries.

Because the Ants are at their Busyness.

Because the Snake poured into its Hole.

Because Weakness and Lone is what becomes of us.

Because no one heard my Voice,
and they must be punished.

Because Sleep is at last.

FRAGMENTS OF THE GOSPEL OF PHILOGELA

A gospel allegedly written by the only woman disciple of Jesus; her name means "laughter-loving". Translated from the Greek papyri found in a sealed urn near the Serbonian bog (Lacus Serbonis) west of al-Arish (Egypt). The texts, which are in a fragmentary state, and in some cases duplicate each other, have been tentatively dated to the seventh century C. E.

The brackets supply material omitted in some copies, or conjectural. Fragment 19 is almost illegible.

1 [...] begins the gospel of Philogela.

2 Jesus said, Philogela, you are a woman; and Greek, and therefore [you are from among the] enemies of my people; but I forgive you, because you follow me and I know that you know me.

The interpretation of this last phrase is disputed.

3 Jesus said, Philogela of Cyprus, feed my sheep [and you shall be fed].

The text in brackets is almost illegible.

4 Jesus was walking with the twelve [and some others]. And Philogela said, Rabbi, here is an inn. Let us go in, for we are weary. Jesus said to [her], The sun also rises, and the stars have their courses; but the Son of Man has nowhere to lay his head. But let us go in, [and eat and drink] for the body labors, and is not unworthy of its hire. — Philogela said, [That seems to me] good.

5 Philogela said, Rabbi, what is the kingdom like [or: to what is it to be compared?] [Jesus said] The kingdom is like a young woman to whom a young man has given his seed.

Her parents and her village were ashamed of her, but [when she gave birth] the son was the wonder of the whole world. — Philogela said, Rabbi, that is a strange teaching.

6 [Jesus said] The kingdom is like a rich king, who taxed his people and gathered their treasure. But when the king grew old and weak, the people rose up and drove him away, and slew his son also, and [they] carried away the treasure; and now all the people have a portion [of that which was] lost. — Philogela then asked Jesus, What was [is] the portion of women? Jesus answered her, The portion of great honor.

7 [Jesus said] The Egyptians worship a beast, and the Indians seek after wisdom; but you have only me, a grain by the wayside. If the rain falls on it, it shall die and be reborn. — Philogela said, I also am a grain...

The papyrus is torn at this point.
Possibly this passage was known to Paul; see I Cor. 1:22.

8 Philogela said, Rabbi, are the rich like us, or do they but have more money? [Jesus said] The stinking camel does not come indoors, and the wealthy have no seat in my Father's house.

9 Philogela said, Rabbi, I still do not understand the kingdom. Jesus said, The kingdom is like the leaves of the walnut tree. When the wind plays with the tree, the leaves wave; and in autumn the nuts fall down, and give food to the poor.

10 Philogela said, Rabbi, I lack wisdom; how shall I find it? [Jesus said] The kingdom [is like] the ostrich in the desert [who] lacks wisdom. The ostrich leaves her egg in the earth, but when the egg hatches, the chick grows, [and] becomes the tallest and swiftest of [all] running birds. — Philogela said, The hen is surely never far from her egg.

See Job 39:13-18.

Philogela said, Men say, I am fond of childish laughter, and am very ignorant. — Jesus said, Samuel was only a child in the temple, but he heard God, while Eli [slept].

Manuscript 11-A has: I am full of nonsense *(phluaria)*. *It adds, at the end:* But I do not deny that you are full of nonsense. *The authenticity of this last sentence has been questioned. It seems to have been written by a later hand.*

12 [Jesus said] The poor work the wheatfields and vineyards, but the owner [thereof] will not pay [them]. But I say unto you, the laborer is worthy of his hire. — Philogela said, The men should refuse to work, and the women should surround the owner's house. Jesus answered [her], That may come to pass.

13 Jesus said, [Take no thought of what you shall eat and drink, but] trust in the Father, for he will provide a table of fish and honey and pure water [and] wine. Philogela said, Rabbi, my feet are tired, with this endless wandering, and I am hungry; when shall that [come to pass]? Jesus said unto her, When the son of the host is slain, then the inn [shall be opened] and the table spread.

The text in brackets is not found in Manuscript 13-B.

Philogela said, The road is dusty, and I am covered [with dust]. Jesus said, When the urn is unsealed, golden dust shall fly out, and blind the eyes of the world. If you have eyes to see, then look and see. Philogela answered him, I need to wash my hair.

Jesus' answer, if any, is illegible.

15 [Jesus said] Eating and drinking, hearing and seeing, teaching and learning, these things shall [all] pass away; but my words shall not pass away.

This is possibly an answer to Philogela, who again would have wanted to know when they would sit down and have a bite to eat, and something to drink. While this is conjectural, it would be consistent with what little we know of the character of Philogela.

16 [Jesus said] Some mount to heaven by the ladder of learning, others [...] love. Philogela said, Rabbi, is not love greater than learning?

Manuscript 16-A has knowledge *(gnosis) in place of* learning *(episteme).*

17 [Simon] Peter said, Philogela, you ply the Rabbi with foolish questions. Jesus said, Simon Peter, leave her in peace [or: let her go in peace]; for God takes the wise in their own craftiness.

See Job 5:13; and also I Cor. 3:19.

18 Philogela said, Rabbi, you have spoken of the kingdom. Jesus said, And I shall speak of it again. Philogela said, Every king hath his councilors; who are [the councilors of] the kingdom? And Jesus answered her, saying, If you wish to be a councilor, you shall be less than a kitchen slave; and if you wish ... [slave?] you shall be a councilor; for the last shall be first, and the first last. Philogela said, Rabbi, I only wish to be a singer in your house. Jesus said, Philogela, it is granted [...]

19 Jesus [...] Philogela [...] truth [...]

[Cetera desunt. *It is not known what happened to Philogela. Some writers say she went to Egypt and built herself a hermitage in the desert; there is also a legend, reported by St. John Psyllos, that she went back to Greece, and died on the island of Cythera. But none of these documents are earlier than the seventh century, and the whole existence of Philogela is conjectural]*.

TO THE HOLY GHOST

Why are you so vaporous, Holy Ghost?
Why are you so hard to locate, Comforter?
Materialize, sir, comfort me with apples.

Appear, Paraclete,
as a young workman, in a clean shirt and jeans,
and bring your girlfriend, in her scalloped-neck blouse,
and tight red skirt.

Let us empty a flagon, us three,
and I will tell you about my woman, far away,

and you will name the highways,
crossing the world,
that you travel,
every day.

LOOKING NORTH, 10° ABOVE THE HORIZON, 18 MARCH 1998

The tree twigs dance
at the window, the sun
light lays its palm
on the plow-tired land.
The dove who-whoops soft
— two kingdoms away.

Be reassured. F
was the note you wanted
on the harmonium, and you played it.
Asteroid number Ten thousand, named Doom!
fades now past Earth, a slowly easting star.

Attend, await. The door of naked morning
is open for you too.

DELAYED ELEGY

(Pablo Neruda, 1904-1973)

They cut off your telephone
before they could get around to
severing your life.

The houses you built, with the dead friends' names
(how grandly!) you scrawled

on those great beams of your three homes, —
the bars, the bottles, the anchor, the wide-
sailing figureheads, carousel horses,
maritime histories, —

all, all! are upended,
tumbled, and plundered,
shut away from your worldfolk.

A thousand shall write on your fence,
that tyranny shall not come near you;
   ... just! because you loved
wooden angels, mariners' compasses, —
simple things that many had handled,

 ... who worked, and sailed,
and carved, and suffered,
but lowly, rarely wrote their own monikers.

I, up here,
who have nothing to offer
(save a bony fragment of Whitman's war poems,
Lincoln's Springfield house, with its horsehair sofa), —

I, had something to add! —
       But your crashing

surf: —

(offshore's mourning populous sundown:
all those long holleracious voices!) —

shouts me
to silence.

SAY OF MY NEIGHBORS

Nor lengthy epitaphs, nor gilded;
but "here they planted, here they builded;
and (most of them) God's holy will did."

4 OCTOBER 1998

The woodstove fire out,
plenty of blankets.
Is that sound an Air Force plane,
inbound to Travis?
or only the old grumbling
long-wandering night-wind?

LINES TO —

I know not why I took
down on this scrap of paper
your name and telephone
number, nay, —
I no longer know
who you are, —

but, dearly beloved
unutterably forgettable
one, kindly give me a call,
and tell me, ere I discard
this document,
why I retain it:

say, "That business about
the pig and the pickup
was all taken care of,
thirty months ago."

If you do this, I shall
be eternally and profoundly
grateful.

Thank you.

WHAT'S NICE ABOUT SPRING

is that girls know when.
Choosing (from shops, catalogs) light dresses,
bermudas, hand-knit sweaters,

they appear! rejoicing!
and, just as white
tulips open
in a warm room,

they smile,
                    just for being smiled at!
                                                    Hey!

Try it, you, it'll work
every time!

And what happens next
is the way of

westwind

REMINDER

"[...]'s poetry does not remind us of abstract painting."
— *a recent quotation.*

If it doesn't remind you of ovening bread —
or the way that your woman rolls over in bed —
just forget about it, dear colleagues:

it's dead.

VERY EARLY IN THE MORNING, 17 FEBRUARY 1999

Crow calls in dense fog.
Almond blossoms just
starting; slowly-uncurling.
My leg pained in sixty-
six-year-old
cold.

But outside:
how tentative the candle-flames
of new white & orange
and just-at-the-thinnest-tip-red!

wild natives of Turkestan:
short-stemmed, —
earliest tulips.

O
THE SUN IS EIG
HT HUNDRED SIXTY
THOUSAND MILES AC
ROSS AND IS ALL PURE
LIGHT AND PURE FIRE
AND PURE SPLENDOR
& PURE SPIRIT &
JOY
!